A MICROWAVE COOKBOOK
JUST FOR KIDS

Kosher Edition

Edited by:
Tamar Peterseil
Dana Porath

Yellow Brick Road Press Ltd.

Table of Contents

KIDS! Read This First...

Cooking with a microwave is fast, easy, and fun. By following the recipes in your **Zap It!** microwave cookbook you'll be able to prepare a dish for yourself, enjoy a snack with a friend, or treat the whole family to an entire meal. But, before preparing the delicious recipes in this book, take a few minutes to read this introduction and learn about cooking in a microwave.

HOW THE MICROWAVE WORKS

When you turn on your microwave, thousands of small waves of energy travel from the sides of the micro-wave into the food. These small, "micro" waves move very quickly in all directions. Their high speed motion zaps the food, causing it to warm up rapidly from the outside-in.

Since the microwave works so quickly, you'll be able to enjoy the original recipes you find in this book in a fraction of the time it would take to prepare them the old-oven way. ➡

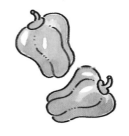

WHAT KINDS OF UTENSILS ARE <u>NOT</u> MICROWAVE SAFE ?

Make sure you use containers, dishes, plates and other utensils that are microwave safe. (It's always best to check with an adult first). Use only glass or porcelain covers to cover the food. Never put metal pots and pans, and utensils with metal, silver or gold trim into your microwave. Never use aluminum foil in a microwave.

TEMPERATURE SETTINGS ON YOUR MICROWAVE

All recipes in this book are designed for a microwave that has 600 watts of power. If your microwave has more -- or less -- than 600 watts of power, refer to the **Zap It!** chart on the facing page.

For example: In "The Delightful Dinosaurs" recipe the potatoes must cook for 6 minutes. Suppose your microwave uses 500 watts of power instead of 600 watts. Find "6 minutes" in the table under the heading "600 watts". Then, move over to the "500 watts" column and you'll find it says 7 minutes. This means you need 7 minutes to cook food it takes 6 minutes to cook in a 600 watt microwave.

If your microwave has only "*high*", "*medium*", and "*low*" settings, use the "*high*" setting for all recipes.

When you try a recipe in this book for the first time, keep the microwave on for a few minutes less than the recipe suggests. That way you can check its progress at one-minute intervals, and, if needed, adjust the recipe to your microwave.

MORE COMPANY... LESS COMPANY

Each recipe tells you how many servings you will be preparing. If you want to double the quantity, simply use twice as many ingredients and **zap** for twice the time. If you want to make only half the amount, use half the amount of each ingredient and **zap** for half the time.

SAFETY FIRST...AND LAST

1) Before you turn on your microwave, close the door securely and make sure the time and temperature controls are set correctly.

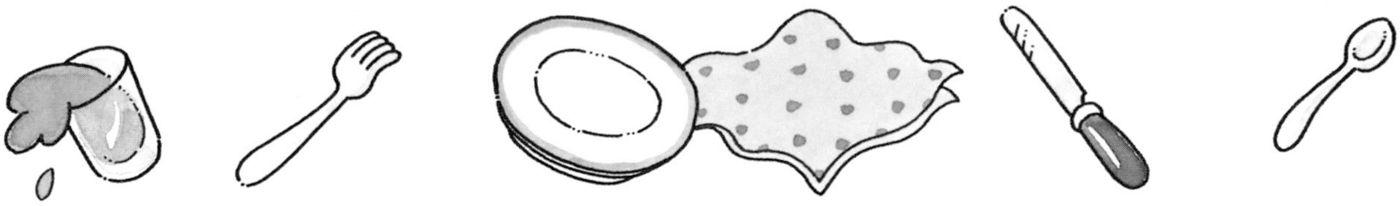

400 Watts	500 Watts	600 Watts	650 Watts	700 Watts
1½ min.	1¼ min.	1 min.	1 min.	1 min.
2¼	2 min.	1½ min.	1½ min.	1¼ min.
3 min.	2½ min.	2 min.	2 min.	1¾ min.
3½ min.	3 min.	2½ min.	2¼ min.	2 min.
4 min.	3½ min.	3 min.	2¾ min.	2½ min.
5½ min.	5 min.	4½ min.	4¼ min.	4 min.
8 min.	7 min.	6 min.	5½ min.	5 min.
14 min.	12 min.	10 min.	9½ min.	9 min.
19½ min.	18 min.	16 min.	14½ min.	13 min.
21¾ min.	19½ min.	17 min.	16 min.	15 min.

2) When you remove a dish from your microwave, be sure to use pot holders or oven mitts to avoid burning your hands.

3) Never open the door of the microwave until the food has stopped cooking and the microwave is turned off.

4) If you have any questions about how to use your microwave or how to prepare a recipe, ask a grownup.

Happy Zapping!

5

Good Morning Toast

Don't wake your parents in the morning, unless you're serving them breakfast in bed. Here's a special treat that's guaranteed to put a smile on even the grumpiest "Who-woke-me-up?" face.

Serves 2:

- 2 slices wholewheat bread
- 1-1/2 tsp. butter
- 2 pear halves (canned)
- 2 tsp. strawberry jam
- 2 slices any hard cheese, including American cheese.

Helpful Hints:

Wait until cheese cools. Then, with a knife, spread some jam over the cheese to make a smiling face.

1 Toast bread and spread butter on it.

2 Drain and slice pears lengthwise.

3 Place pears on bread and spread jam over them.

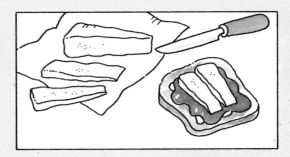

4 Slice cheese into strips. Place the strips over pears and jam.

5 Put toast on a plate and *zap* in microwave for 1-1/2 minutes or until cheese melts.

Bart's Eary Sandwich

Check out the Bart hairstyle and those outlandish ears! Here's a sandwich you and your friends will enjoy creating and eating. The original faces in this picture are hanging in The Museum of Modern Bart.

Serves 2:

- 2 slices wholewheat bread
- 2 globs ketchup
- 4 slices tomato
- 2 strips green pepper for face
- 2 strips red pepper for face
- 2 strips carrots for face
- 1 tsp. oil
- 4 slices American cheese
- Salt, pepper, oregano to taste

Helpful Hints:

Make a face on the cheese before your put it into the microwave. Be creative, be daring... be Bart!

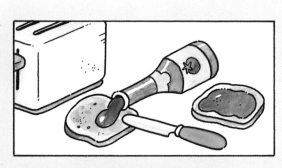

1 Toast bread and spread 1 glob of ketchup on each slice.

2 Place oil, peppers, and carrots into bowl. Cover bowl and *zap* in microwave for 4-1/2 minutes.

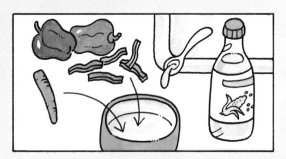

3 Place 2 slices of cheese on each slice of toast.

4 Carefully remove peppers and carrots from bowl and place on cheese. Slide the tomato slices under the cheese.

5 Sprinkle salt, pepper and oregano.

6 Put the toast on a plate and *zap* in microwave for 3 minutes.

Top This

Some tomatoes are so ripe their tops just pop right off. These lid-poppers usually have a delicious surprise inside them. Something most people just wouldn't expect from a tomato...unless they know this recipe.

Serves 2:

- 2 tomatoes
- 1/4 lb. chopped meat
- 1/2 cup cooked rice
- 2 tsp. fresh chives
- Salt and pepper to taste

Helpful Hints:

Cook rice before starting recipe. See rice package for instructions.

To decorate add a few strips of yellow or green pepper. Serve with lettuce or spinach leaves.

1 Wash tomatoes, remove and SAVE tops.

2 Remove seeds with a spoon.

3 Mix rice, chopped meat, salt, pepper, and chives in a bowl. Stuff meat mixture into tomatoes.

4 Put tomatoes on plate and *zap* for 2 minutes in microwave.

5 Replace tops and re-*zap* tomatoes 2 more minutes in microwave.

6 Decorate with lettuce, peppers or spinach leaves.

Magic Meat Loaf

You need the right magic words to make this recipe. "Egggogone" usually does it. But be careful. If you don't have just the right accent all the eggs in the meatloaf may disappear...and reappear in the soup!

Serves 4:

- 5 fresh eggs
- 1/2 tsp. pareve margarine
- 3 slices stale bread
- 2 medium onions, cubed
- 1-1/2 lbs. chopped meat
- 1 tbs. salt
- 1 tsp. paprika
- 1 tsp. pepper

Helpful Hints:

In order to puncture the shell of an egg you need either a needle or an "egg puncturing" utensil. When you puncture the eggs, it is easier to peel off the shells after they are cooked. However, this step is optional.

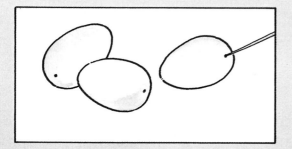

1 Puncture 3 eggs. *(See Helpful hints.)*

2 Boil the 3 eggs on the stove for 6 minutes on medium heat.

3 Smear margarine in loaf dish.

4 Dip bread in cold water and let drain.

5 Mix bread, onions, chopped meat, 2 fresh eggs, and spices into bowl and fashion into loaf in loaf dish.

6 Peel hard boiled eggs and insert them into meat loaf mixture.

7 Put meat loaf in microwave and *zap* for 16 minutes.

8 Remove from microwave and let sit for 10 minutes. Slice it up. Who's got the eggs?

Funny-Face Soup

Smile! You're on Candid Camera! This delicious soup makes you take a good look at yourself. Some people have trouble with this recipe (for obvious reasons). Others just eat it up.

Serves 2:

- 10 oz. frozen peas
- 2-1/2 cups water
- 4 tsp. pareve powdered bouillon
- 2-1/2 tbs. milk
- 1 tsp. sugar
- 1 tsp. salt
- 2 sprigs of parsley

Helpful Hints:

Slice some carrot and radish rings to make a self-portrait. Corn kernels make great eyeballs and a radish or a cherry tomato is the perfect nose. Now ...smile!

1 Put the peas, water, and bouillon in a large bowl.

2 Stir, cover, and *zap* in microwave for 10 minutes.

3 Remove from microwave. Blend with electric mixer or blender for 2 minutes.

4 Add milk, sugar, and salt.

5 Divide soup into two bowls and re-*zap* in microwave for 1 minute.

6 With the parsley, carrots, radishes and corn, make a face in the soup as shown above.

Delightful Dinosaurs

These tummy tinglers make great "Guardosaurs". Put them in your stomach before you go to bed and you'll feel safe all night. They've been known to polish off a stray Pterodactyl or Tyrannosaurus Rex in no time.

Serves 2:

- 2 large potatoes
- Aluminum foil to wrap potatoes
- 1 yellow pepper strip for eyes
- 4 radish rings for ears
- 2 strips red pepper for tongue
- 8 strips carrots for feet
- 2 small pickles for tail

Helpful Hints:

Be careful not to tear the aluminum foil when you put the vegetable pieces into the potatoes.

Slice yellow pepper strip into 4-6 pieces.

1 Wash potatoes unpeeled.

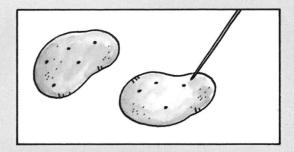

2 Prick potatoes several times with a wooden toothpick.

3 *Zap* potatoes in microwave for 6 minutes.

4 Remove potatoes from microwave. Wrap each potato in aluminum foil and let sit for 5 minutes.

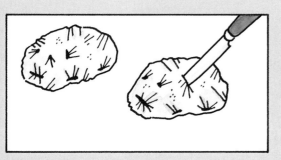

5 Make holes in aluminum foil with knife for ears, eyes, feet, tongue and tail.

6 Gently push the pickles, radishes, peppers, and carrots into the holes as shown above.

Vegetable Helper

Some kids don't like to eat their vegetables. Sally is one of them. So she concocted this terrific schnitzel recipe. She takes one bite of schnitzel, and eats one pea. A second bite of schnitzel and eats two peas. A third bite of schnitzel, and eats four peas....It works with carrots too.

Serves 2:

- 10 oz. turkey breast
- 1/2 tsp. salt
- 1/2 tsp. curry
- 1/2 tsp. ginger
- 1/2 tsp. powdered cloves

- 1 tsp. honey
- 3 tsp. lemon juice
- 2-1/2 tsp. mustard
- 1 medium size can of mixed vegetables

1 Rinse the turkey and dry with paper towel.

2 Mix salt, curry, ginger, cloves, honey, lemon juice, and mustard in a bowl.

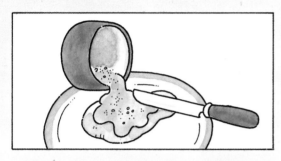

3 Place turkey on plate. Pour mixture from bowl over turkey.

4 *Zap* turkey in microwave for 6 minutes. Remove plate.

5 Place vegetables on a separate plate and *zap* in microwave for 4 minutes.

6 Decorate turkey with vegetables.

Lickety Split

It pays to go on a diet just so you can dig into this scrumpdelicious banana split. If you should need to gain a little weight try two of these. Sally once ate three and we couldn't even draw her on a full page!

Serves 2:

- 2 scoops ice-cream
- 2 bananas
- 1/2 tsp. sugar
- 1 bar chocolate(1.55 oz.)
- 3-1/2 tsp. whipped cream

Helpful Hints:

Ready for adventure? You can set sail by peeling the rind of an orange and spearing it onto the banana with a toothpick.

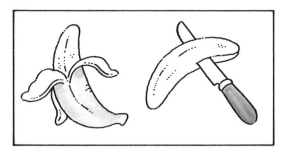

1 Peel bananas and slice lengthwise.

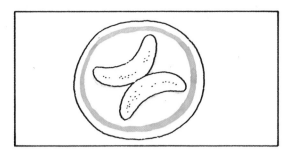

2 Place the two halves of the banana on a dish, side-by-side, as shown.

3 Break chocolate bar into small pieces.

4 Place the sugar, chocolate, and whipped cream into a bowl and mix well.

5 *Zap* in microwave for 1 minute. Remove bowl.

6 Mix sauce well. Place scoop of ice cream on center of banana halves.

7 Pour the chocolate sauce over the bananas.

Berry Good

Kevin prepared this especially for Mark and Debra, who have come to celebrate his birthday. But, since they both chipped in to buy only one present, Kevin decided to eat two portions, while Mark and Debra will have to share one serving. Fair is fair.

Serves 2:

- 10 oz. raspberries
- 4 tsp. sugar
- 4 small scoops ice cream

Helpful Hints:

Put some of your favorite fruits around the ice cream. A cookie rising out of one of the scoops makes this even more delectable.

1 Liquify raspberries in mixing bowl using an electric mixer or blender.

2 Add sugar to raspberry sauce and mix well.

3 Place sauce in microwave and *zap* for 2 minutes.

4 Put 2 scoops of ice cream on each plate.

5 Pour sauce over ice cream and decorate.

Warning! Mousse Loose!

What's the plural of moose? Mousse? Well, actually there is no plural for moose, probably because they only appear one at a time. But happily, there is a plural for mousse. Here it is...

Serves 2:

- 3 chocolate bars(1.55 oz. each)
- 5 tbs. sour cream
- 2 egg yolks
- 2 egg whites
- 1 tbs. vanilla sugar
- 1 tsp. sugar

Helpful Hints:

For a non dairy mousse, substitute pareve whipped cream for sour cream, and pareve semi-sweet chocolate for mllk chocolate.

When the mousse is done, top with whipped cream, bits of fruit, some nuts and your favorite topping.

1 Place chocolate bars and sour cream in large dish.

2 *Zap* in microwave for 20 seconds. Stir well. Re-*zap* for 20 seconds. Stir well. Re-*zap* again for 20 seconds. Stir well.

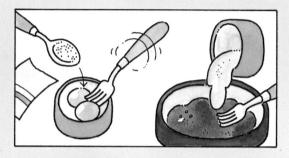

3 Beat egg yolks and vanilla sugar in bowl. Add to chocolate mixture and mix for one minute.

4 Beat egg whites and sugar until stiff.

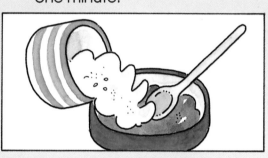

5 With a large spoon, mix egg whites with chocolate mixture.

6 Put mousse in 2 dessert bowls. Cool in refrigerator for 2 hours.

Cheers! A Kid's Cocktail

Drinking and hammocking don't mix. Some kids just can't hold their grape juice. So, be careful about giving this recipe to a younger brother or sister. Kevin drank some in his hammock...and promptly flipped right over!

Serves 2:

- 1-1/4 cups pure orange juice
- 4 tsp. lemon juice
- 3/4 cup purple grape juice
- 3/4 cup white grape juice
- 2 orange slices
- 6 red cherries
- 6 green grapes

Helpful Hints:

To give this drink a more professional look, take two swizzle sticks or long toothpicks and follow steps 3-5.

For a tingling, different taste, substitute grapefruit juice for orange juice.

1 Mix orange, lemon and grape juices into pitcher. Stir. Pour into 2 glasses.

2 *Zap* drinks in microwave for 2 minutes. Remove and stir.

3 Spear 3 grapes and 3 cherries on each swizzle stick as shown. Put one stick in each glass.

4 With a knife, cut two orange slices from the middle of an orange. Split each slice as shown.

5 Hang the slices over the edge of each glass.

Miracle Milk

This recipe helps build strong bodies. We guarantee you'll love the taste of it. Especially, if you are into body building. Sally's bear had a sip and he's on his 37th sit-up!

Serves 2:

- 3 tsp. honey
- 1-1/4 cups milk
- 2 egg yolks
- 4 tbs. caramel topping

Helpful Hints:

If this recipe is too healthy for you, drink it with your favorite cookies.

1 Mix honey, milk, and topping into a bowl or small glass pitcher.

2 **Zap** milk mixture in microwave for 2 minutes.

3 Pour 2 teaspoons of the hot milk mixture into the egg yolks. Stir well.

4 Pour egg yolks into remaining milk mixture. Stir again.

5 Pour into two glasses and sprinkle with cinnamon.

Happy Birthday Surprise!

Kevin never brings presents to his friends' birthday parties. He bakes the cake. That way he is sure to get the biggest piece. Best of all, after the party's over, Kevin takes home what's left.

Serves 4:

- 1 tsp. butter for oiling dish
- 1 large can pineapple chunks
- 4 eggs
- 2 cups milk
- 1 tbs. sugar
- 2 tsp. vanilla or 1/2 vanilla stick
- 14 hard round biscuits
- 1 tbs. butter for icing
- pinch of cinnamon

Helpful Hints:

Decorate the cake with cherries or fruits.

If you're really daring you might pour on some chocolate fudge topping, especially on the piece you've reserved for yourself!

1 Smear teaspoon butter on a large baking dish. Drain canned pineapple chunks.

2 Mix eggs, milk, sugar and vanilla in a bowl.

3 Place 7 biscuits in baking dish.

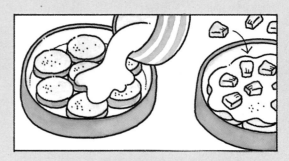

4 Pour half of mixture from step 2 on biscuits. Put a layer of pineapple on top.

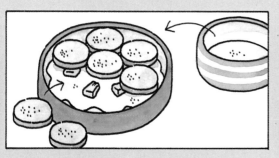

5 Place remaining biscuits over the pineapple. Pour on remaining mixture.

6 Place small pieces of butter around top of entire mixture. Sprinkle with cinnamon.

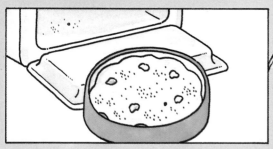

7 **Zap** in microwave for 17 minutes.

Etc.

Cooking Terms:

Beat - stir vigorously
Cubed - chopped into small pieces
Glob - a little more than a "shmear" - see page 9
Pareve - having no milk or meat ingredients
To taste - according to how you like your food seasoned

Abbreviations

lb. - pound
oz. - ounce
tbs. - tablespoon
tsp. - teaspoon

How to separate egg whites:

Gently crack the egg on the rim of a glass. Separate the shell halves slowly. Keep the yolk in one half of the shell. Pour the white from the other half of the shell into a small bowl. Slide the yolk into the empty half shell. Pour any leftover egg white into bowl. Put yolk into the second bowl.